T4-ADO-809

Date: 4/20/22

J 398.21 HAM
Hamilton, Sue L.,
The world's scariest zombies

XTREME SCREAMS

THE WORLD'S SCARIEST
Zombies

A&D Xtreme
BOLD HI-LO NONFICTION
An imprint of Abdo Publishing
abdobooks.com

S.L. HAMILTON

TAKE IT TO THE XTREME!

GET READY FOR AN XTREME ADVENTURE! THE PAGES OF THIS BOOK WILL TAKE YOU INTO THE THRILLING WORLD OF THE SCARIEST ZOMBIES ON EARTH. WHEN YOU HAVE FINISHED READING THIS BOOK, TAKE THE XTREME CHALLENGE ON PAGE 45 ABOUT WHAT YOU'VE LEARNED!

ABDOBOOKS.COM

Published by Abdo Publishing, a division of ABDO, PO Box 398166, Minneapolis, Minnesota 55439. Copyright © 2022 by Abdo Consulting Group, Inc. International copyrights reserved in all countries. No part of this book may be reproduced in any form without written permission from the publisher. A&D Xtreme™ is a trademark and logo of Abdo Publishing.

Printed in the United States of America, North Mankato, MN.
032021
092021

THIS BOOK CONTAINS RECYCLED MATERIALS

Editor: John Hamilton; Copy Editor: Bridget O'Brien
Graphic Design: Sue Hamilton
Cover Design: Laura Graphenteen
Cover Photo: iStock

Interior Photos & Illustrations: Activision-pgs 42-43; Alamy-pgs 14-15; AMC-pg 41 (top); Crown Publishers-pg 37 (top); Dover Publications-pg 34; EC Comics-pg 38 (top); Getty Images-pgs 11, 19 & 26-27; Image Ten-pg 40 (zombie hands); iStock-pgs 1, 10, 12-13, 16-17, 22-23, 32-33, 34-35 (bkground), 36 (lineart), 36-37 (bkground) & 44; Granger-pgs 8-9; Marvel Entertainment-pgs 38 (bottom) & 39; Mary Evans-pgs 24-25; Minden-pg 18; Parmount Pictures-pg 37 (bottom); PopCap Games-pg 43 (top); Science Source-pgs 28-29 & 30-31; Shutterstock-pgs 4-5, 6-7 & 20-21; Sourcebooks Young Readers-pg 35 (bottom); The CW-pg 41 (bottom); Three Rivers Press-pg 36 (book); Two Lions-pg 35 (top); Universal Pictures-pg 40.

LIBRARY OF CONGRESS CONTROL NUMBER: 2020948019

PUBLISHER'S CATALOGING-IN-PUBLICATION DATA

Names: Hamilton, S.L., author.

Title: The world's scariest zombies / by S.L. Hamilton

Description: Minneapolis, Minnesota : Abdo Publishing, 2022 | Series: Xtreme screams | Includes online resources and index.

Identifiers: ISBN 9781532194894 (lib. bdg.) | ISBN 9781644946275 (pbk.) | ISBN 9781098215200 (ebook)

Subjects: LCSH: Zombies--Juvenile literature. | Zombies in popular culture--Juvenile literature. | Zombies in mass media--Juvenile literature. | Zombie films--Juvenile literature. | Zombie television programs--Juvenile literature. | Zombies in literature--Juvenile literature. | Monsters--Juvenile literature.

Classification: DDC 398.2454--dc23

TABLE OF Contents

THE WORLD'S SCARIEST ZOMBIES 4
HISTORY 6
ZOMBIE CREATORS 10
MAKING A ZOMBIE 16
ZOMBIE SIGHTINGS 24
REAL ZOMBIES 28
HOW TO KILL A ZOMBIE 32
ZOMBIES IN THE MEDIA 34
ARE SUPERNATURAL ZOMBIES REAL? 44
XTREME CHALLENGE 45
GLOSSARY 46
ONLINE RESOURCES 47
INDEX 48

CHAPTER 1
THE WORLD'S SCARIEST Zombies

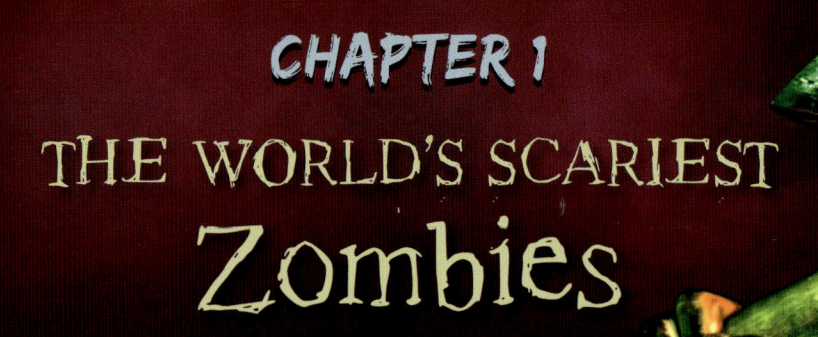

Zombies are walking corpses. They have died but have been awakened through supernatural means. The rotting **cadavers** seek out the living, intent on killing and eating the humans they find.

XTREME FACT

In many horror stories, zombies want to eat human brains.

CHAPTER 2

History

The term zombie may have come from the African word *nzambi*, or "god." The Grand Serpent (*Le Grand Zombi*) was the father of all loas, or gods. He appeared in the shape of a large python. Dangerous and unpredictable, this loa could only be controlled by a strong **bokor** or **black magician**.

7

African slaves brought **voodoo** (also called vodou) to French plantations on the island of **Haiti** in the 1700s. Owners tried to stop the religion by punishing or killing the **houngans** and **bokors**. These practitioners began to use their powers in secret. Their **black magic** was said to cause illness, death, and even to turn people into zombies.

XTREME FACT

Haitian slaves came to the United States through trading centers in Louisiana and South Carolina. Some brought their voodoo practices with them. A few became well-known for their powers.

A New Orleans, Louisiana, voodoo ceremony.

CHAPTER 3
Zombie Creators

New Orleans, Louisiana, has been the center of **voodoo** practices since the 1700s. People of all colors, wealthy and poor, called on voodoo kings and queens to use their powers for **curses**, cures, and love potions. Some were said to create zombies.

Voodoo kings and queens used a variety of objects for their black magic, including chicken feet and blood.

Some people feared the strange, supernatural voodoo religion, while others were drawn to it.

Dr. John Montenet was a famous **voodoo** priest. He was a tall, heavily tattooed man of color. Many people thought his powers were real.

Dr. John kept human and animal bones, snakes, toads, scorpions, herbs, and charms. He used these items, and others shown here, to make traditional African medicines.

Dr. John owned slaves, and several were thought to be zombies he created. He was said to send his zombie slaves to local cemeteries to dig up and steal corpses.

Marie Laveau was known as a **voodoo** queen in New Orleans in the early 1800s. People paid for her fortune-telling, as well as charms and **curses**. Many wives asked Marie to help with unfaithful husbands. Although the famous queen is not known to have turned any men into zombies, she did become famous for her voodoo ceremonies. She danced with Le Grand Zombi—a giant snake.

XTREME FACT

Marie was once a hairdresser. She learned many secrets about people in this job. She also paid local servants to keep her informed. She knew what was going on in the city, and this helped her tell fortunes that proved true.

Marie Laveau

CHAPTER 4
MAKING A Zombie

How do people become zombies? Modern scientists have studied the powders and potions used by **voodoo** practitioners.

XTREME FACT
A single puffer fish has enough poison to kill 30 adults. However, certain parts of the fish are edible when prepared by an experienced chef.

Puffer fish are known to contain a deadly **toxin** called tetrodotoxin. Eating the eyes and internal organs of a puffer fish may result in paralysis and death. Given in small doses, it may have been used to create zombies.

A cane toad has glands behind its head that produce a highly toxic poison. The milky white fluid from the toad may have been used to sicken and control victims.

A cane toad oozes a poisonous fluid when it feels threatened.

XTREME FACT

There are stories of humans dying from the cane toad's poison. However, it is usually an unfortunate animal, such as a dog or cat, that bites the toad and dies.

Hyla tree frog

The Hyla tree frog is another **amphibian** that oozes a toxic liquid. The substance won't kill, but it may open tiny sores on a human's skin. It is through these openings that a **voodoo** master might place a poison to create a zombie.

A powerful magician may make people think they are zombies.

While drug potions may turn people into the walking dead, scientists believe that it is the power of suggestion that finishes the spell. If people believe they have been zombified, it seems real. Most likely it's a combination of poisons together with the words of a powerful magician that creates zombies.

If bitten by a zombie, a human must quickly leave other humans before the infection turns that person into one of the undead.

22

In many **fiction** stories, a bite from a zombie will turn a human into the walking dead. Once bitten, it takes only a short time for the infection to spread. A victim may turn into a zombie in only minutes.

CHAPTER 5
Zombie Sightings

Felicia Felix-Mentor of **Haiti** died and was buried in 1907. However, 30 years later she stumbled into her village. Some thought she was a zombie. Others believed it might be someone claiming to be Felicia.

XTREME FACT

It's a crime to turn someone into a zombie in Haiti. So if someone is drugged, buried as if dead, then dug up and brought back to life, it is still considered murder in Haiti.

Felicia Felix-Mentor believed she had been turned into a zombie.

Clairvius Narcisse died on May 2, 1962, in **Haiti**. Doctors issued a death certificate and his family saw him buried. In 1980, Narcisse walked up to his sister. He had been a zombie slave on a sugar plantation until his master's death.

Narcisse sits at the Haiti cemetery site where he was buried in May 1962.

Narcisse died because he did not want to sell some land that he and his brothers owned. They arranged for him to be poisoned. He seemed dead. After his burial, he was dug up and revived by a zombie master who kept him drugged for years. Narcisse did not return to his village until all the brothers who had caused his terrible life had died.

CHAPTER 6
Real Zombies

A skin condition known as yaws makes people look like zombies. Yaws causes open sores on the sufferer's face, legs, arms, and feet. The painful wounds on the bottoms of the feet sometimes cause a sufferer to walk in a slow, zombie-like shuffle.

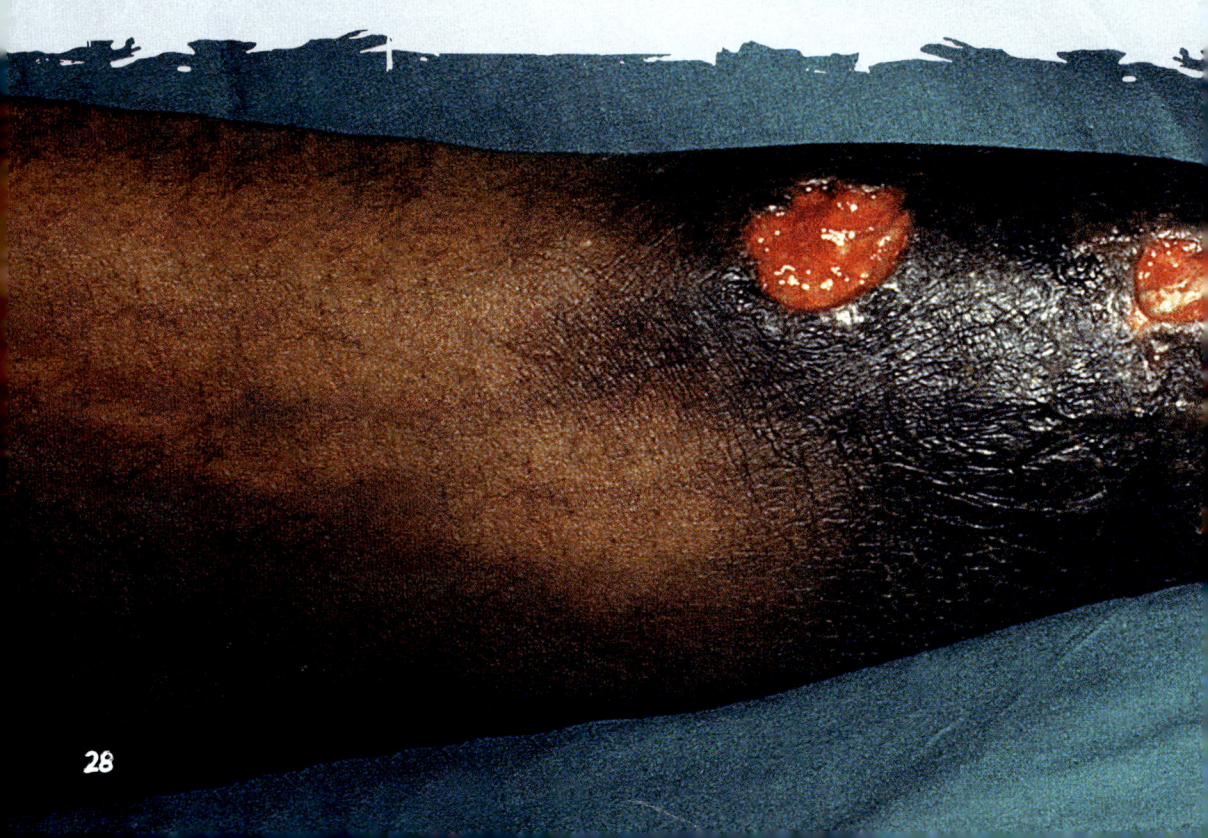

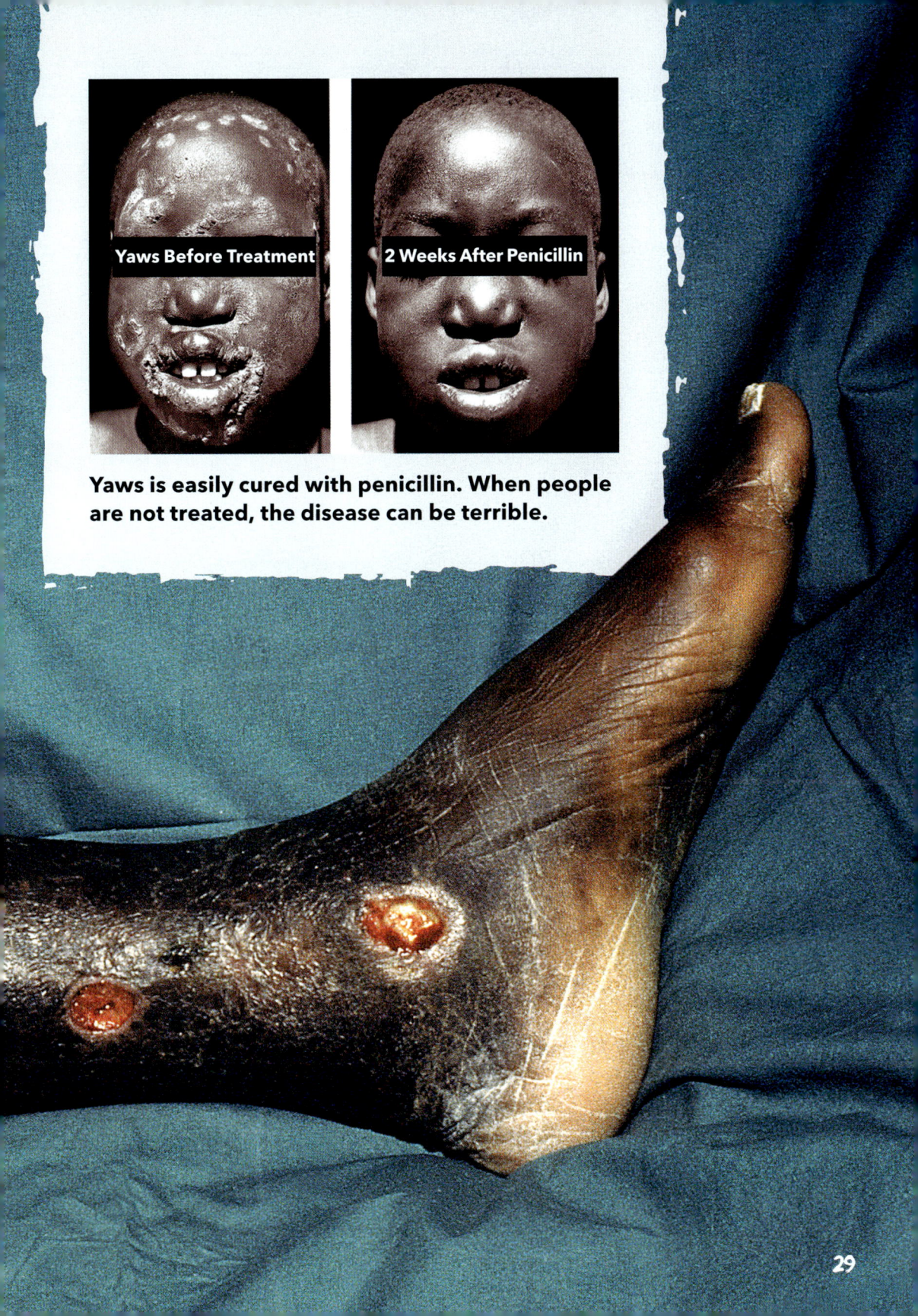

Yaws Before Treatment **2 Weeks After Penicillin**

Yaws is easily cured with penicillin. When people are not treated, the disease can be terrible.

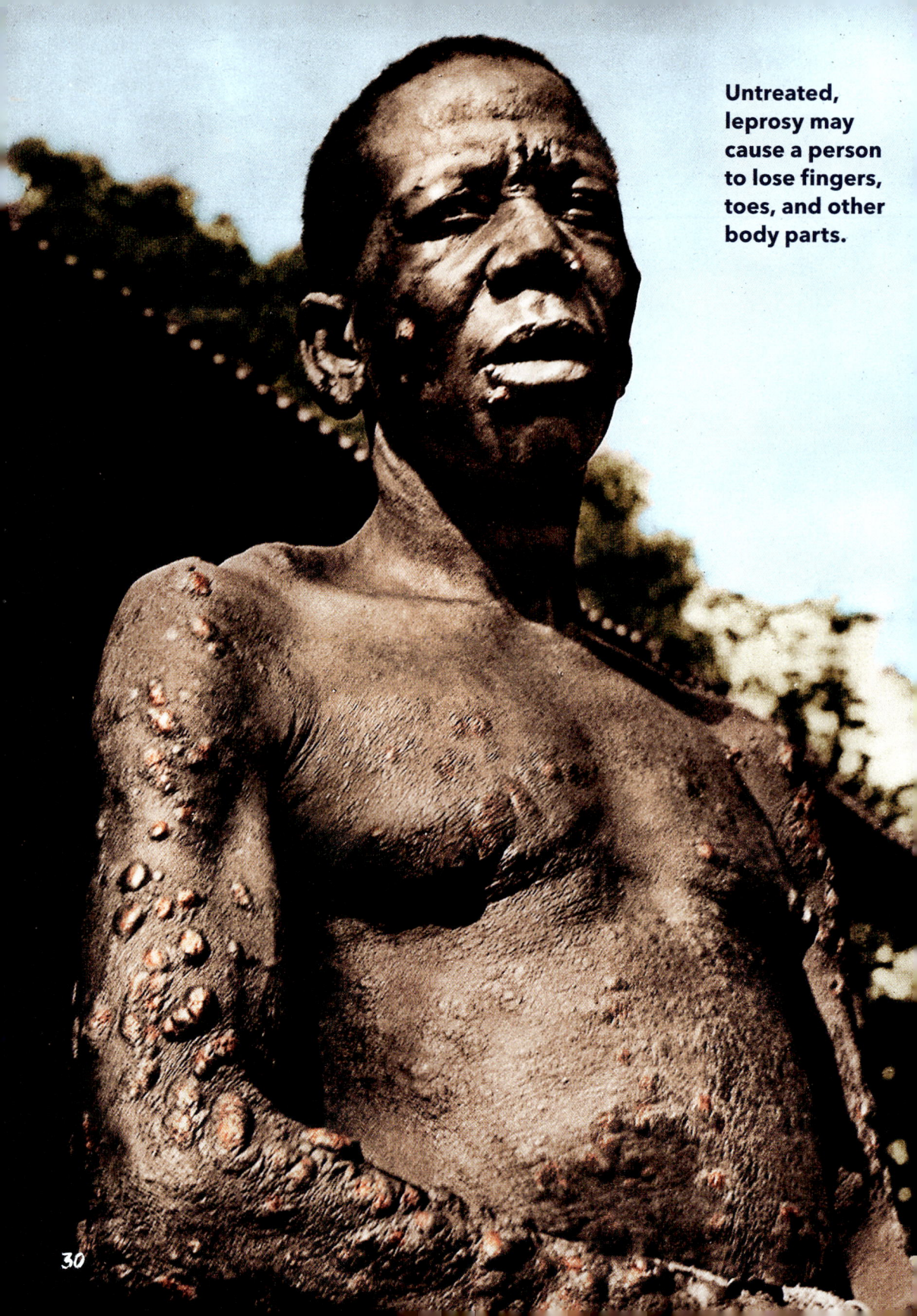

Untreated, leprosy may cause a person to lose fingers, toes, and other body parts.

Leprosy also **mimics** some of the conditions of zombies. The medical condition causes sores and **decay** of body parts. Modern drugs have cured millions of leprosy patients.

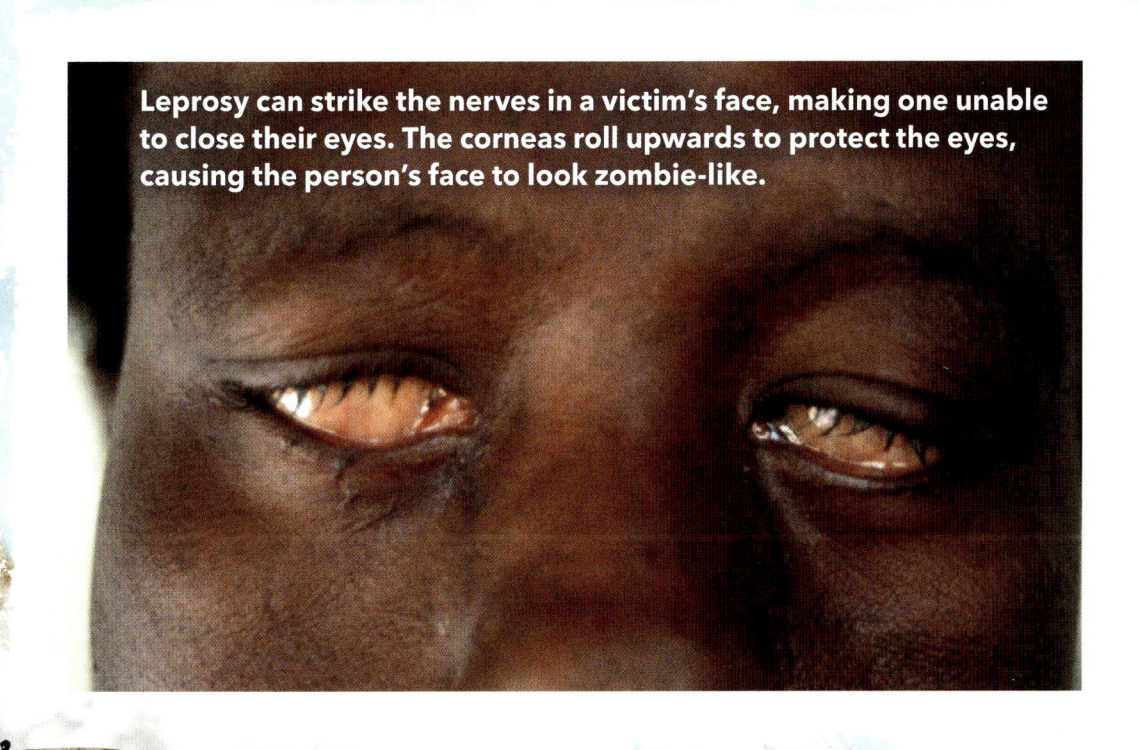

Leprosy can strike the nerves in a victim's face, making one unable to close their eyes. The corneas roll upwards to protect the eyes, causing the person's face to look zombie-like.

XTREME FACT

About 95% of the world is naturally immune to leprosy.

CHAPTER 7
HOW TO KILL A Zombie

Most legends say that to kill a living corpse, one must destroy its brain. That means cutting off the head or hitting it with a bat or a brick. Some zombie hunters destroy the whole body by burning it or using explosives.

XTREME FACT

Since zombies are actually walking corpses, they feel no pain when they are killed (again).

CHAPTER 8
Zombies In the Media

Zombies are popular creatures in horror tales. *The Magic Island* was one of the first zombie stories. William Seabrook told of his experiences in **Haiti** with practitioners of **black magic** and **voodoo** in his 1929 book. Many exciting zombie **fiction** stories followed.

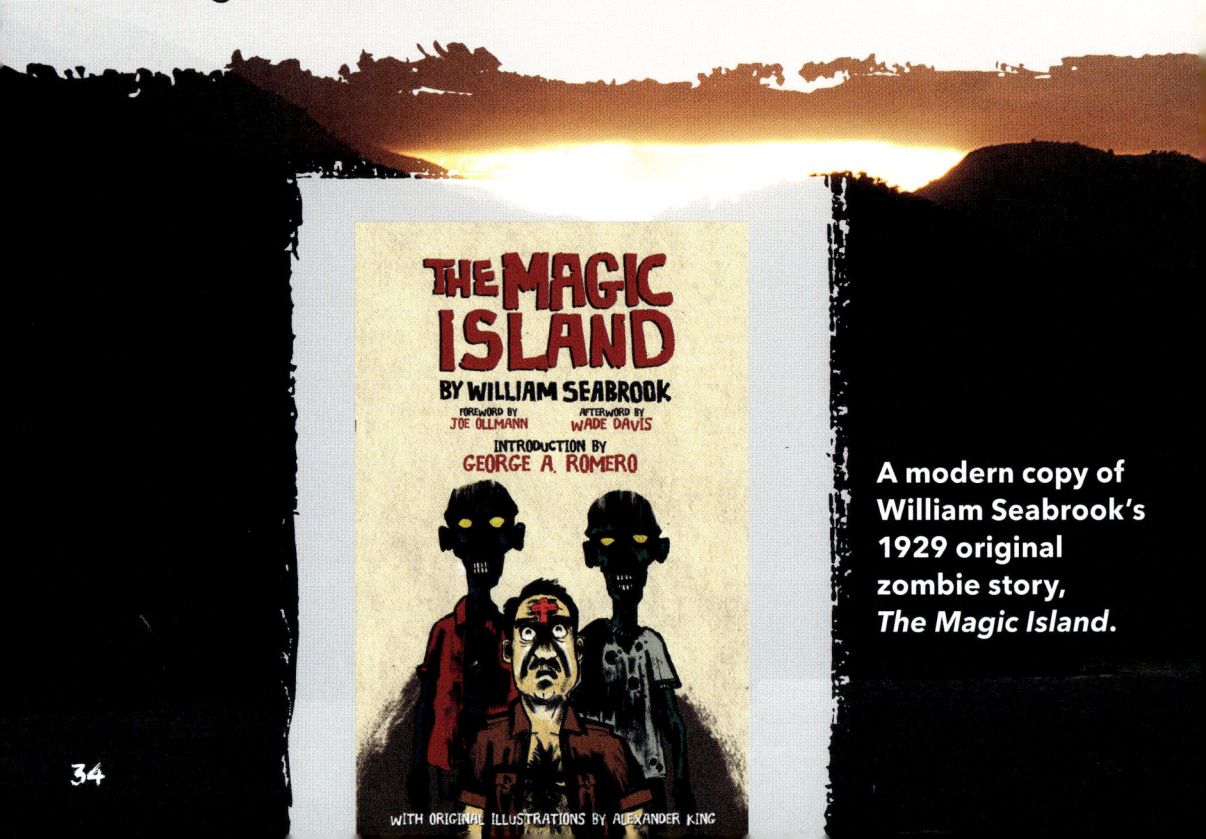

A modern copy of William Seabrook's 1929 original zombie story, *The Magic Island*.

R.L. Stine's *Zombie Town* features kids at a horror movie where the zombies come alive and attack.

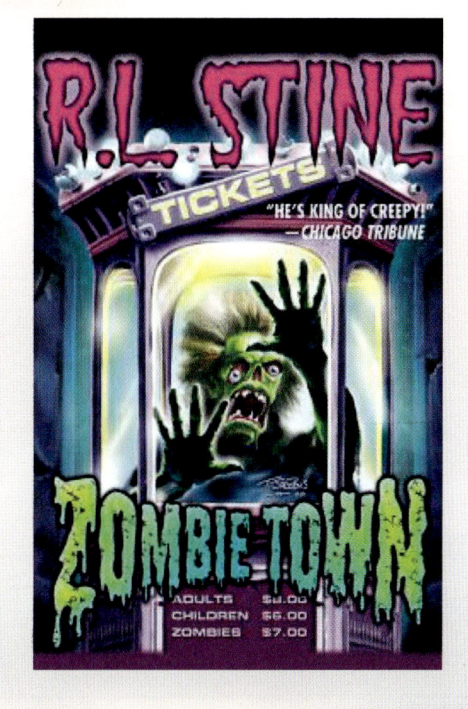

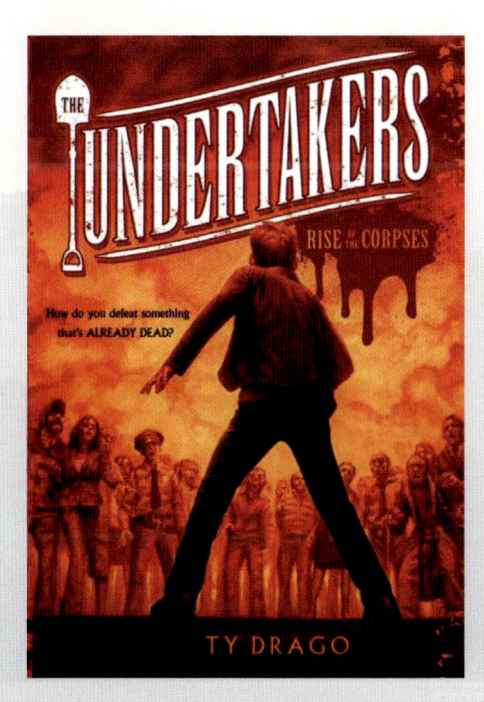

In Ty Drago's *The Undertakers* an army of teen fighters take on walking corpses.

Max Brooks wrote some of the most famous zombie books. *The Zombie Survival Guide* and *World War Z* talk about zombie plagues and what could happen on Earth. *World War Z* also became a movie and a video game.

A worldwide infection creates deadly zombies in Max Brooks's *World War Z.*

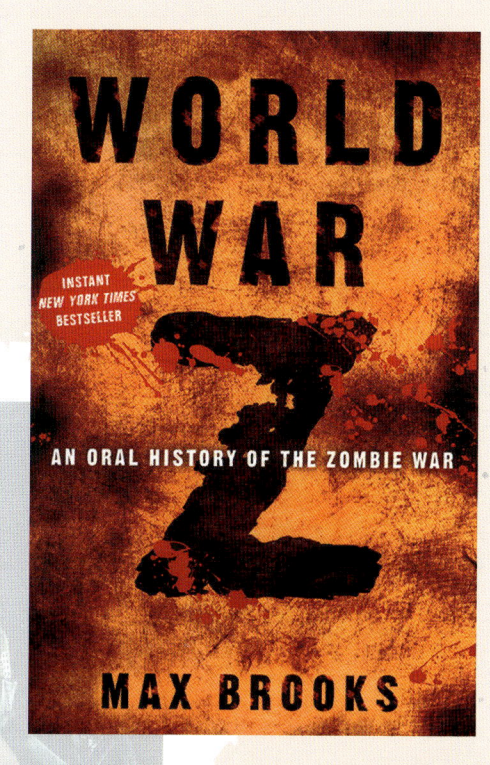

For decades, comic books have used the walking dead to create great graphic horror stories. The frightening possibility of anyone turning into a zombie makes for terrifying tales.

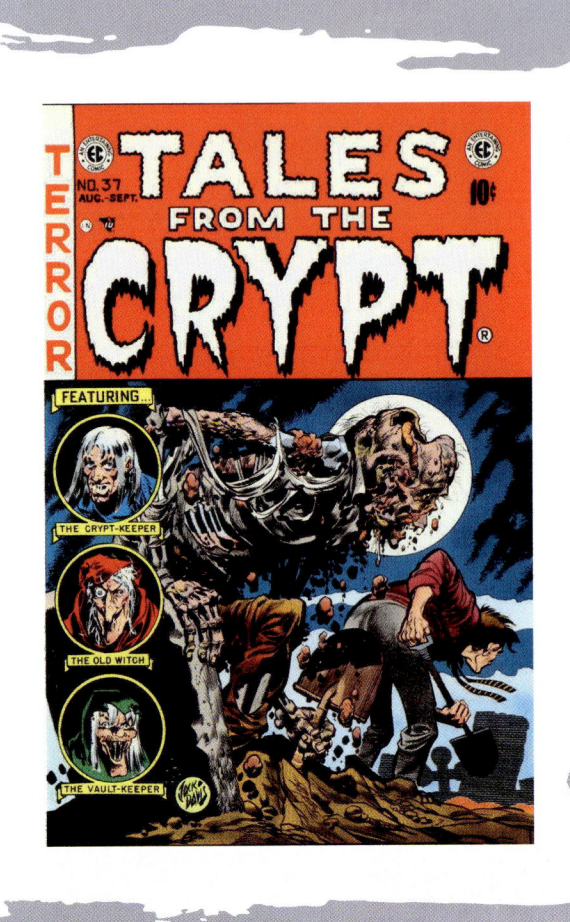

In *Marvel Zombies*, the powerful superheroes become infected with a virus from outer space. They are hungry for flesh and brains but still try to save Earth from an invasion.

The gruesome look of zombies made them popular in horror comic books, such as the 1950s *Tales from the Crypt* series.

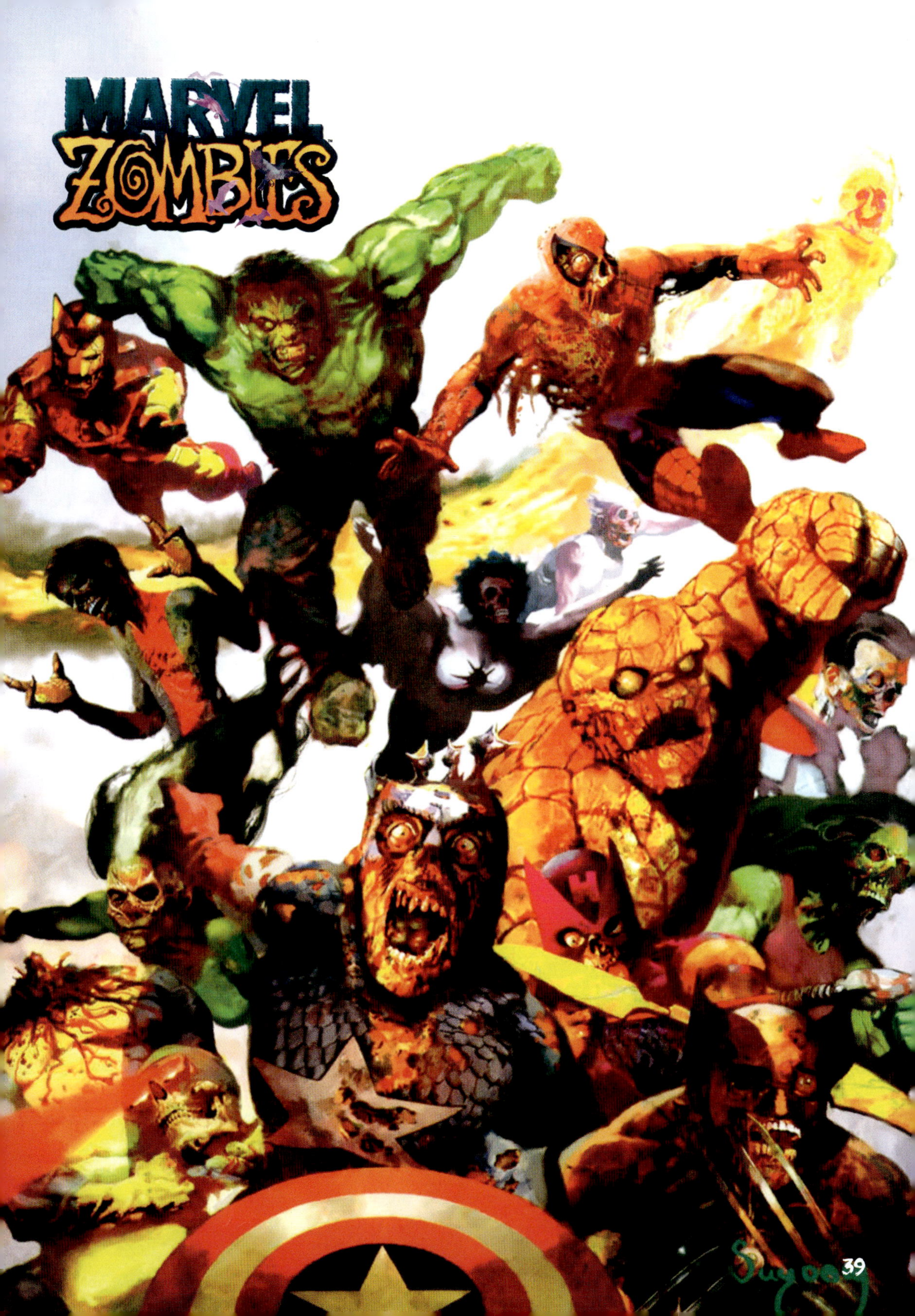
MARVEL
ZOMBIES

A London salesman is surrounded by zombies in *Shaun of the Dead*. The movie was inspired by several horror films, including Romero's *Night of the Living Dead* series.

***Night of the Living Dead* was the first of a series of six zombie horror films.**

The most well-known zombie movies are from director George A. Romero's *Night of the Living Dead* series. The first movie was released in 1968. Sequels and re-makes have continued for more than 50 years. Zombie comedies such as *Shaun of the Dead* and the *Zombieland* series have brought laughs and horror.

40

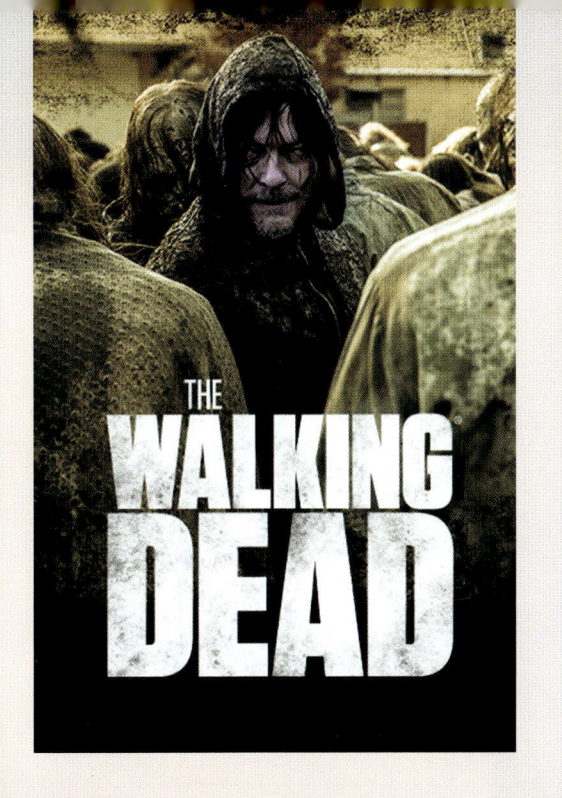

Survivors face off against zombie "walkers" in the popular TV series *The Walking Dead*.

TV shows such as *The Walking Dead*, *iZombie*, and *Ash vs. Evil Dead* have become popular zombie thrillers.

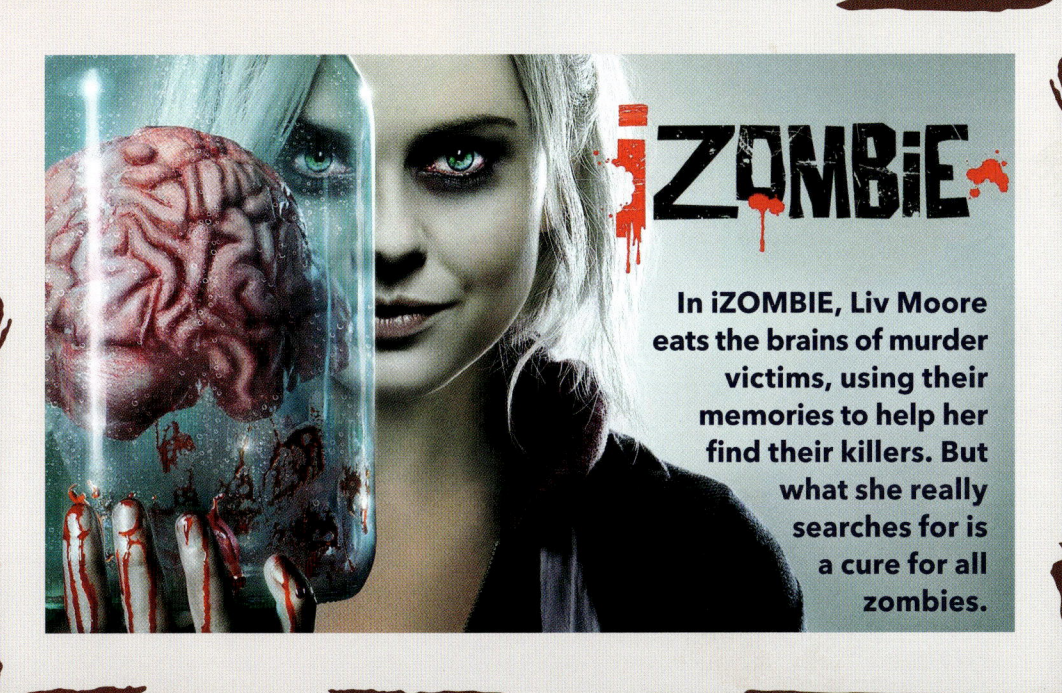

In iZOMBIE, Liv Moore eats the brains of murder victims, using their memories to help her find their killers. But what she really searches for is a cure for all zombies.

Zombie-themed games can be gruesome and fun. Players often fight attacking zombies, but sometimes a person plays as a zombie. Zombies often have supernatural powers, and can bite, hit, and vomit on their enemies.

In one game mode of *Call of Duty: World at War*, players face off against zombies.

In *Plants vs Zombies: Garden Warfare*, players may control the plants or the zombies.

43

CHAPTER 9
ARE SUPERNATURAL ZOMBIES Real?

Zombies aren't real, but authors, makeup artists, and actors create terrifying **fictional** monsters with dead eyes, **decaying** skin, and frightening shuffles. In real life, it's drugs, powerful suggestions, and medical conditions that make people appear to be the walking dead.

XTREME Challenge

TAKE THE QUIZ BELOW AND PUT WHAT YOU'VE LEARNED TO THE TEST!

1) In fiction, what do zombies want to eat?

2) What kind of creature was Le Grande Zombi?

3) What Caribbean island became the center of zombie lore in the 1700s?

4) What religion seemed to give practitioners the ability to turn people into zombies?

5) What is the name of a famous voodoo queen who lived in New Orleans in the early 1800s?

6) Name three creatures that have toxins or poisons that may have been used to create zombies.

7) Name two medical conditions that may cause a sufferer to look like a zombie.

8) In fiction, how are zombies killed?

Glossary

amphibian – A class of animals that includes frogs, newts, toads, and salamanders.

black magic – Magic that is practiced with the purpose of doing evil or causing harm to someone.

bokor – A practitioner of black magic capable of creating zombies.

cadaver – A dead body, a corpse.

curse – A series of words or a wish for something bad to happen.

decay – To rot or decompose. Usually, the tissue of once-living things, such as humans, animals, and plants, begins to decay as soon as they die.

fiction – Stories that are made up by a writer or speaker. Not fact.

Haiti – An island in the Caribbean. It was a busy slave center in the 1700s.

houngan – A male priest in the voodoo religion.

mimic – To do something the same way as something or someone else does it.

toxin – Something that causes living things to sicken and sometimes die.

voodoo – Also called vodou. A religion begun in Haiti by slaves brought from Africa. It combines elements of many religions and uses rites from several ethnic groups. One type of voodoo includes the practice of zombification.

Online Resources

Booklinks NONFICTION NETWORK
FREE! ONLINE NONFICTION RESOURCES

To learn more about the world's scariest zombies, please visit **abdobooklinks.com** or scan this QR code. These links are routinely monitored and updated to provide the most current information available.

Index

A
African, 6, 8, 12
Ash vs. Evil Dead, 41

B
black magic, 6, 8, 10, 34
bokor, 6, 8
Brooks, Max, 36, 37

C
Call of Duty: World at War, 42
cane toad, 18

D
Drago, Ty, 35

E
Earth, 36, 38

F
Felix-Mentor, Felicia, 24, 25

G
Grand Serpent, 6

H
Haiti, 8, 9, 24, 26, 34
houngan, 8
Hyla tree frog, 19

I
iZombie, 41

L
Laveau, Marie, 14, 15
Le Grand Zombi, 6, 14
leprosy, 30, 31
loa, 6
London, England, 40
Louisiana, 9, 10

M
Magic Island, The, 34
Marvel Zombies, 38, 39
Montenet, John, 12, 13
Moore, Liv, 41

N
Narcisse, Clairvius, 26, 27
New Orleans, LA, 9, 10, 14
Night of the Living Dead, 40

P
Plants vs Zombies: Garden Warfare, 43
puffer fish, 16, 17

R
Romero, George A., 40

S
Seabrook, William, 34
Shaun of the Dead, 40
South Carolina, 9
Stine, R.L., 35

T
Tales from the Crypt, 38
toxin, 17

U
Undertakers, The, 35
United States, 9

V
voodoo, 8, 9, 10, 11, 12, 13, 14, 16, 19, 34

W
Walking Dead, The, 41
World War Z, 36, 37

Y
yaws, 28, 29

Z
Zombie Survival Guide, The, 36
Zombie Town, 35
Zombieland, 40